Dorcas
Sews for Others

Acts 9:36-42 FOR CHILDREN

Written by Alberta Poth Miller
Illustrated by Susan Morris

ARCH Books

ST. LOUIS, MISSOURI 63118
MANUFACTURED IN THE UNITED STATES OF AMERICA
ISBN 0-570-06184-2

Dorcas lived in a town by the sea,
Where the waves rolled high and the wind blew free.
Ships sailed in and out every day
Bringing in goods from lands far away.

While many merchants were well-dressed and rich,
There were many poor people with scarcely a stitch
To cover their backs and keep them warm
In the evening's chill or the winter's storm.

Old folks were walking around
in rags;
Their clothes were like faded
and tattered bags.
The children, too, had little to
wear,
And what they had was in
need of repair.

Dorcas watched, and she thought, "Some day
I'll help these people; I'll find a way,
For that is what Jesus would want me to do,
And with His help I can do it, too."

Dorcas knew how to sew extremely well,
And those who knew her could always tell
Which clothes she had made or mended with care.
In sewing her talent was beyond compare.

She searched for material both high and low.
Then with needle and thread she began to sew
New clothes for those that were tattered and torn,
New clothes for those that were faded and worn.

How pleasant to see an old gray head
    Covered with a bright-colored mantle instead
Of rags that let the cold air through
    To chill old bones and cause pain, too.

How good Dorcas felt when she saw the joy
    That shone in the face of a girl or boy
To whom she had given a new robe or cloak.
    What a joy it was to help the poor folk!

Then one day kind Dorcas became very sick.
People tried to help her get better real quick.
They tried all they knew, and many cried,
For they couldn't help her, and Dorcas died.

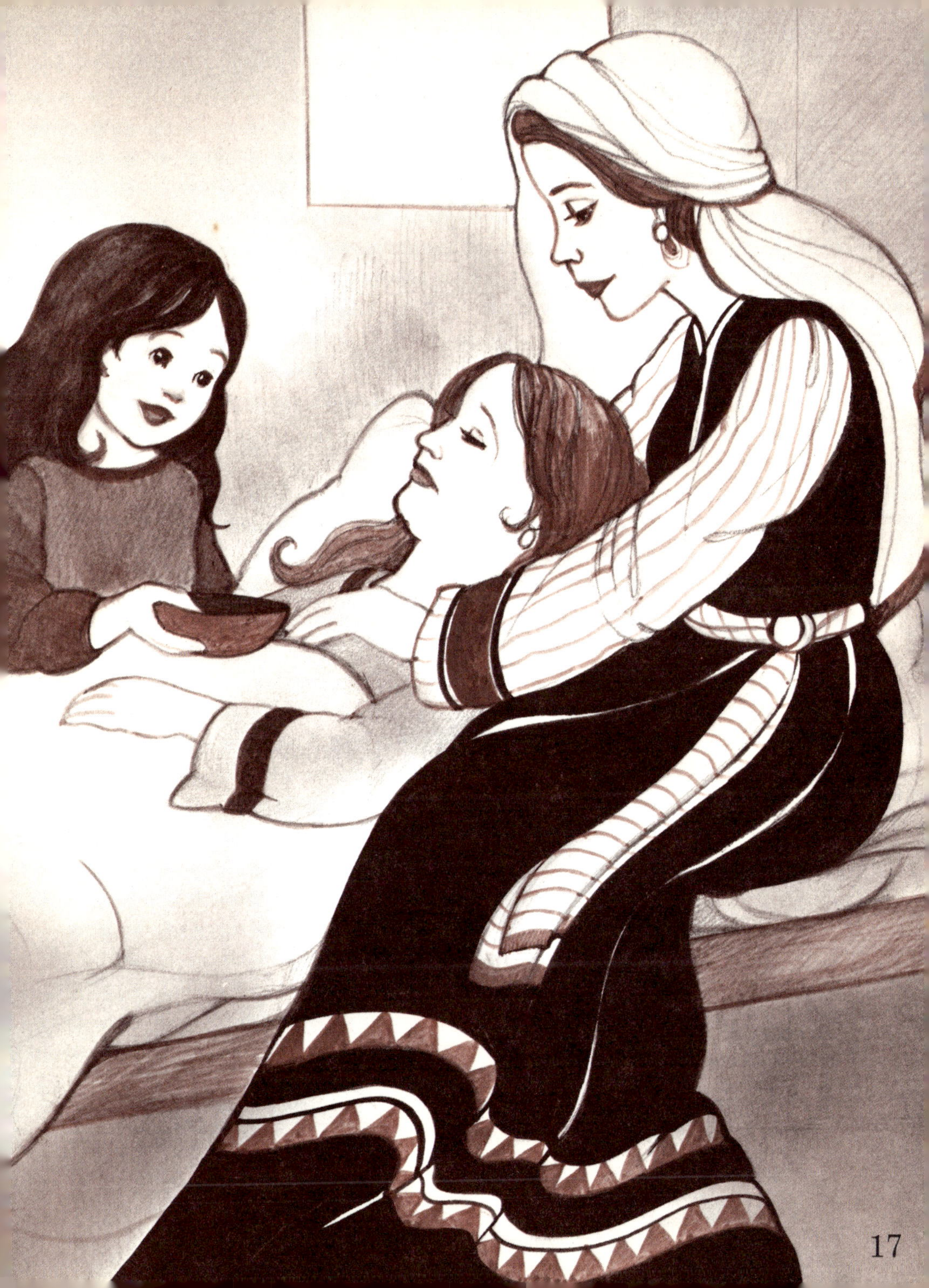

“What will we do?” the poor people said,
“For we still need clothes, and Dorcas is dead.
How we’ll miss this lady, so wonderfully kind!
People like Dorcas are hard to find.”

Then someone remembered that Peter was near
In a town close by and would want to hear.
They knew that he was Jesus’ friend, too,
But Dorcas was dead, so what could he do?

But still they sent two messengers down
To try to find Peter in the nearby town.
They soon found Peter, who was preaching there;
They told him of Dorcas and hoped that he'd care.

Peter came at once and saw the great pain
In the eyes of those who had helped her in vain.
He went to her room and looked down on the bed
Where Dorcas was lying so cold and dead.

Peter turned to the people, who were filled with gloom,
And asked everybody to leave the room.
Then he prayed to Jesus in heaven above
And asked Him to help Dorcas, out of His love.

Peter took Dorcas' hand, so still on her bed,
And using her Hebrew name instead,
"Tabitha," he said to her, "Arise,"
And Dorcas sat up and opened her eyes.

The people were glad more than tongue can tell
That Jesus, through Peter, had made Dorcas well.
They gave thanks to Jesus in grateful prayers
For this kind little lady who really cares.

Then Dorcas, having been raised from the dead,
Once again picked up her needle and thread
And began to sew robe, mantle, and cloak
To gladden the hearts of the poorest folk.

We, too, can help others if we aren't shy.
God's love for us makes us want to try.
He gives us the things that we can do,
And when we try, He helps us, too.

Like Dorcas we must understand
And always lend a helping hand,
And spread our sunshine every day
By helping others in every way.

DEAR PARENTS:

The Book of Acts gives us a number of examples of the way in which followers of Jesus, who came to be called Christians, carried out the Lord's call to "love your neighbor as yourself." That became the natural way of life for those who knew His love and were changed by it. It was so natural that Christians became known in their communities as the people who loved one another.

Dorcas was just one example of an active, loving disciple (follower of Jesus' teachings). Her story is brief but powerful. She "was always doing good and helping the poor" (Acts 9:36 NIV). She made a tremendous impact on those she helped. Undoubtedly, she led some to know the Lord through her service. Even more persuasive was the dramatic way in which God restored her to those she helped.

There is a great need today also for people who "love because he first loved us" (1 John 4:19 NIV). As your children read about Dorcas's service to others long ago, encourage them in the same way of life with examples they can see today.

THE EDITOR